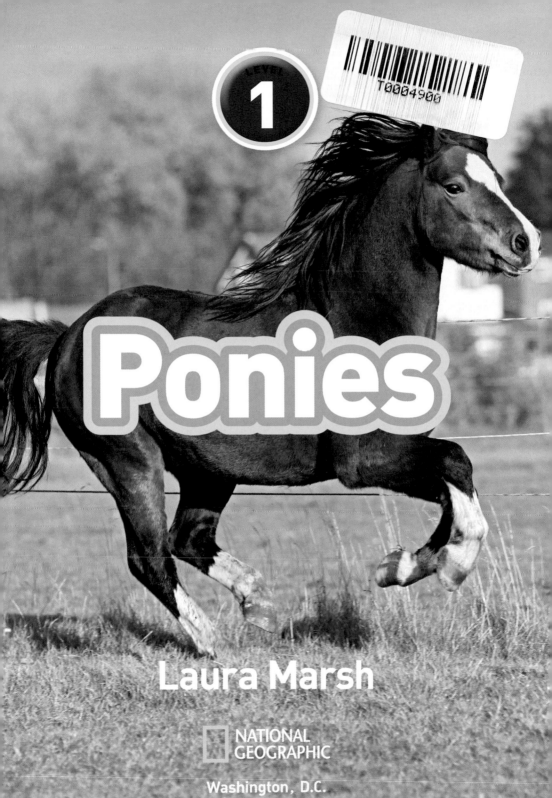

LEVEL **1**

Ponies

Laura Marsh

NATIONAL GEOGRAPHIC

Washington, D.C.

For Alec
—L.F.M.

Design by Yay Design

Trade Paperback ISBN: 978-1-4263-0849-9
Library Binding ISBN: 978-1-4263-0850-5

Photo credits: Cover, Philip Tull/Oxford Scientific/Photolibrary.com; top border of the page (throughout), Dennie Cody/Getty Images; 1, Zuzule/iStockphoto; 2, Tim Graham/The Image Bank/Getty Images; 4–5, Gallo Images/Getty Images; 6, Eric Isselée/Shutterstock; 7 (UP LE), Ocean/Corbis; 7 (UP RT), Image Source/Corbis; 7 (LE CTR), Mikhail Kondrashov/iStockphoto.com; 7 (RT CTR), Lenkadan/Shutterstock; 7 (LO LE), Eduard Kyslynskyy/Shutterstock; 7 (LO RT), Daniel Gale/Shutterstock; 8, Jane Burton/naturepl.com; 9, Fionline digitale Bildagentur GmbH/Alamy; 10–11, Cornelia Doerr/Photographer's Choice/Getty Images; 11, ARCO/naturepl.com; 12 (LE), Kristel Richard/naturepl.com; 12 (RT), blickwinkel/Alamy; 13 (UP LE), Juniors Bildarchiv/Alamy; 13 (UP RT), Rachel Faulise; 13 (LO LE), Foto Grebler/Alamy; 13 (LO RT), Zuzule/Shutterstock; 14 (UP LE), teamtime/iStockphoto.com; 14 (UP RT), pastoor/iStockphoto.com; 14 (LO LE), Andries Oberholzer/Shutterstock; 14 (LO RT), Matti/Alamy; 15 (UP LE), Zuzule/iStockphoto; 15 (UP RT), enis izgi/iStockphoto.com; 15 (LO LE), Oshchepkov Dmitry/Shutterstock; 15 (LO RT), Lagui/Shutterstock; 16 (LE), Geoff du Feu/Photodisc/Getty Images; 16 (RT), Tim Burrett/NationalGeographicStock.com; 17 (UP LE), Frank Lukasseck/Photographer's Choice/Getty Images; 17 (UP RT), Kim Tegg/National Geographic My Shot; 17 (LO LE), Mikhail Kondrashov "fotomilk"/Alamy; 18–19, Steve Cicero/Corbis; 20–21, Flickr RF/Getty Images; 22, Hulton Archive/Getty Images; 22 (background), Torkile/iStockphoto.com; 23, Jack Delano/Hulton Archive/Getty Images; 24–25, Westend61/Getty Images; 25 (UP), Dorling Kindersley/Getty Images; 25 (CTR), Dorling Kindersley/Getty Images; 25 (LO), Lynn Johnson/NationalGeographicStock.com; 26, Medford Taylor/National Geographic/Getty Images; 27 (UP), Danny Smythe/iStockphoto.com; 27 (RT CTR), Borodaev/Shutterstock; 27 (LE CTR), Juniors Bildarchiv/Alamy; 27 (LO), Michael Westhoff/iStockphoto.com; 27 (UP LE), Ben Molyneux Sports/Alamy; 28 (UP), Nicole Gordine/Shutterstock; 28 (CTR RT), Dorling Kindersley/Getty Images; 28 (LO LE), Timothy Large/Alamy; 28 (LO RT), Dorling Kindersley/Getty Images; 29, Blue Destiny/Alamy; 30 (LE), Anja Hild/iStockphoto.com; 30 (RT), Iurii Konoval/iStockphoto.com; 31 (UP LE), Igumnova Irina/Shutterstock; 31 (UP RT), Charles Mann/iStockphoto.com; 31 (LO LE), jadimages/Shutterstock; 31 (LO RT), Sian Lewis/iStockphoto.com; 32 (UP LE), Rachel Faulise; 32 (UP RT), Steve Cicero/Corbis; 32 (LO LE), Jane Burton/naturepl.com; 32 (LO RT), Ocean/Corbis

National Geographic supports K–12 educators with ELA Common Core Resources.
Visit natgeoed.org/commoncore for more information.

Printed in the United States of America
18/WOR/6

Table of Contents

It's a Pony!

Ponies are special animals. They are beautiful and strong. They are kind and loyal. They like to be around people and other animals.

What Is a Pony?

A pony is a kind of horse.

Horses and ponies are measured in hands. Ponies are 14.2 hands or shorter.

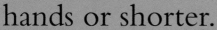 = equals four inches

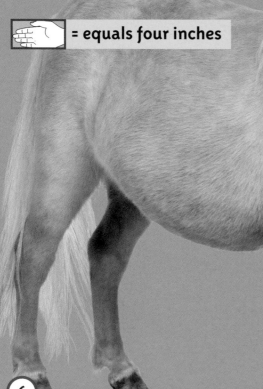

Horse   Pony

L E G S

long legs

short legs

B O D Y

sleek body

wide body

H E I G H T

tall

short

A Foal Is Born!

Pony Word

MARE:
A female horse

It's springtime. A mare gives birth to a baby pony. The baby is called a foal. Welcome, little one!

A foal can stand soon after birth.
It is wobbly on its feet at first.

The foal will run and play before long

All ponies are called foals in the first year.

Young female ponies are called fillies.

Young male ponies are called colts.

11

Pony Breeds

There are many kinds of ponies all over the world.

Some pony breeds have been around for many, many years. Others are newer breeds.

Section A Welsh Mountain Pony

Exmoor Pony

Dartmoor Pony

Assateague Pony

Connemara Pony

Norwegian Fjord Pony

Colors and Markings

palomino

spotted

blue roan

chestnut

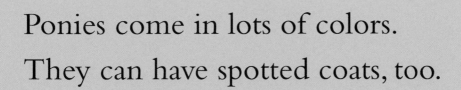

Ponies come in lots of colors.
They can have spotted coats, too.

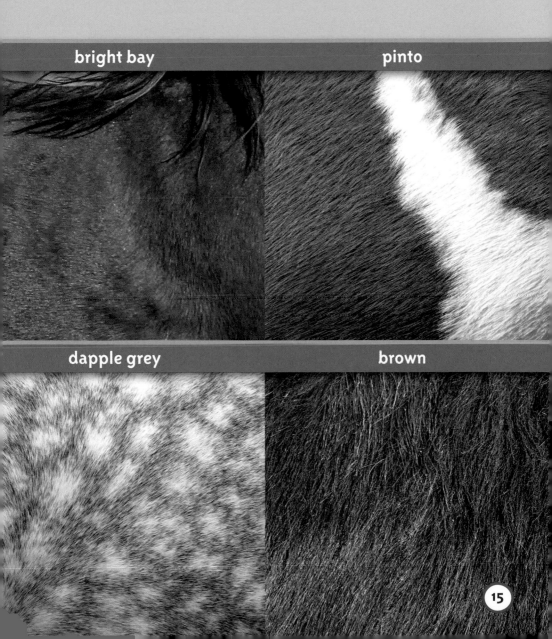

bright bay

pinto

dapple grey

brown

15

Some ponies have white patches of hair. These are called markings.

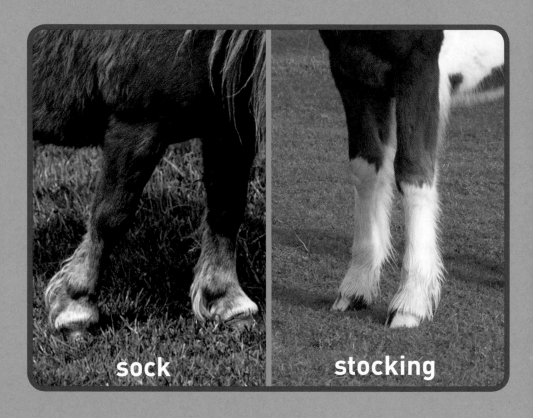

sock

stocking

A pony's feet can have a sock or stocking.

blaze

star

A pony's head can have a blaze, a star, a snip, or a stripe.

snip

stripe

Wild Ponies

There are still wild ponies today.

A herd of wild ponies lives in Maryland and Virginia, U.S.A.

They are called the Chincoteague and Assateague ponies.

Chincoteague?
Say *SHING-keh-teeg*

Assateague?
Say *AS-seh-teeg*

Pony Word

HERD: A large group of animals that live together

The herd has been around for more than 500 years!

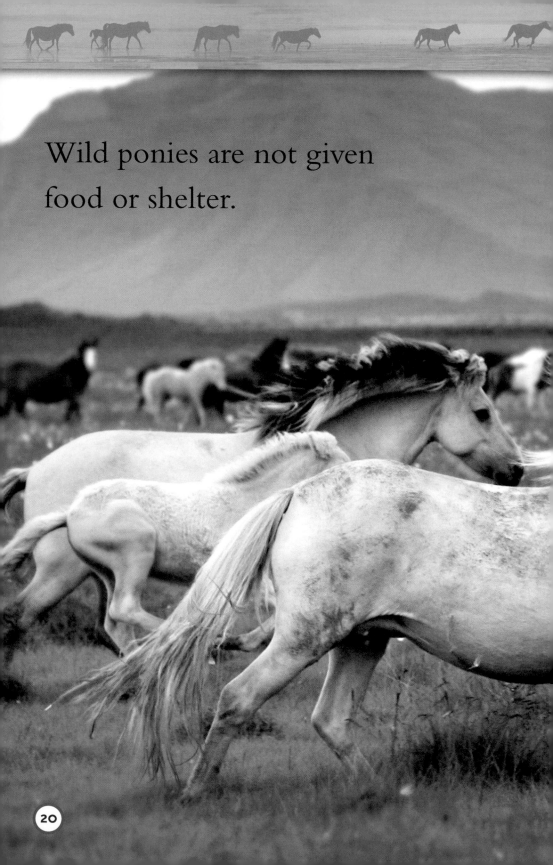

Wild ponies are not given
food or shelter.

They run free.

21

Pony Word

SHELTER:
A safe place
that gives
protection from
bad weather

Ponies in the Past

Ponies in the past were used for work.

Ponies pulled carriages around town. They carried people and things.

pony-drawn carriage

coal mine pony

Ponies also worked on farms, in the mountains, and in coal mines.

Ponies Today

Ponies today are still used for work.

But mostly people ride and enjoy them.

People ride ponies in shows and races. They ride ponies on trails.

They even ride them on vacations.

Caring for a Pony

Ponies make great pets.
But they are a lot of work!

Every day a pony needs fresh food and water, exercise, brushing, and cleaning.

27

Riding

The work is done. Now it's time to ride!

riding helmet

You will need special clothes. The clothes protect you and the pony.

riding pants called jodhpurs

Jodhpurs? Say *JOD-purrs*

gloves

riding boots

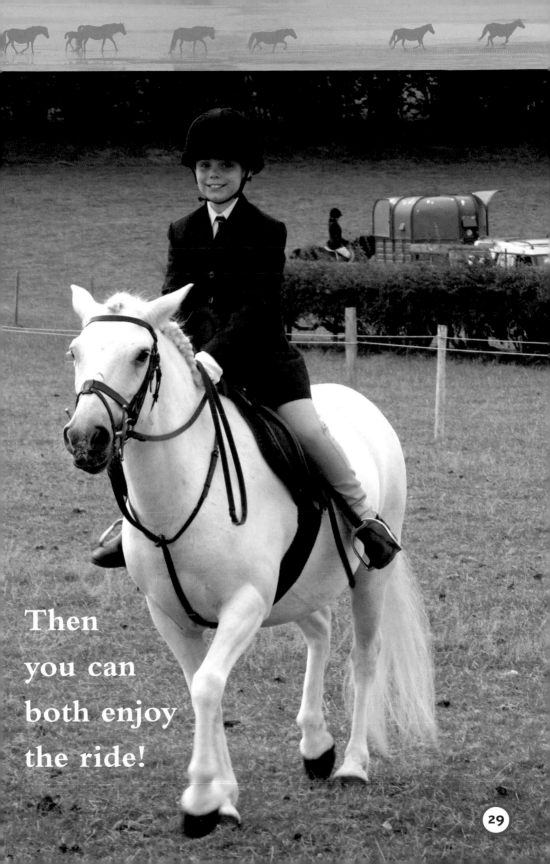

Then
you can
both enjoy
the ride!

What in the World?

These pictures show close-up views of pony things. Use the hints below to figure out what's in the pictures. Answers on page 31.

1

2

HINT: This pony marking rhymes with "gaze."

HINT: A pony rider sits here.

WORD BANK

mane	blaze	helmet	saddle	star	foal

3

HINT: A baby pony is called this for the first year.

4

HINT: You need to wear this when you ride.

5

HINT: A pony's neck has this long hair.

6

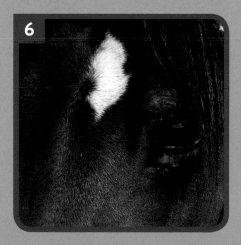

HINT: This pony marking rhymes with "car."

Answers: 1. blaze, 2. saddle, 3. foal, 4. helmet, 5. mane, 6. star

BREED: A group of animals that have similar features and look alike

HERD: A large group of animals that live together

MARE: A female horse

SHELTER: A safe place that gives protection from bad weather

LEVEL
2

Pandas

Anne Schreiber

NATIONAL GEOGRAPHIC

Washington, D.C.

For Lee Lee and Indy

Paperback ISBN: 978-1-4263-0610-5
Hardcover ISBN: 978-1-4263-0611-2

Cover, 6, 13, 18 left, 19 right, 28-29 (all),: © Lisa & Mike Husar/ Team Husar Wildlife Photography; 1, 22: © Katherine Feng/ Minden Pictures/ National Geographic Stock; 2, 32 (top, right): © WILDLIFE GmbH/ Alamy; 5: © Keren Su/ China Span/ Alamy; 6 (inset): © James Hager/ Robert Harding World Imagery/ Getty Images; 8-9, 32 (top, left): © DLILLC/ Corbis; 10-11: © Eric Isselée/ Shutterstock; 14: © age fotostock/ SuperStock; 16, 24-25: © Katherine Feng/ Globio/ Minden Pictures/ National Geographic Stock; 17, 18-19, 32 (bottom, left): © Katherine Feng/ Minden Pictures; 21: © Kent Akgungor/ Shutterstock; 22-23 (inset), 32 (middle, right): © Carl Mehler/ National Geographic Society, Maps Division; 26, 32 (bottom, right): © ChinaFotoPress/ Getty Images; 30-31 (all): © Dan Sipple; 32: (middle, left): © Kitch Bain/ Shutterstock.

Special thanks to Kirsten Speidel, Assistant Professor of Chinese Language, Swarthmore College, for help with translation and pronunciation.

**National Geographic supports K-12 educators with
ELA Common Core Resources.
Visit www.natgeoed.org/commoncore for more information.**

Table of Contents

Giant Panda!

Look! Up in the tree!
Is it a cat? Is it a raccoon?
No! It's a **Giant Panda!**

Giant Pandas can climb to
the tops of the tallest trees.
They live in the highest
mountains. They munch on
bamboo for hours each day.

Bear Cat

Giant Panda ——————•

Black Bear

Pandas are about the same size as their black bear cousins, but their heads are larger and rounder. Also, pandas cannot stand on their hind legs like other bears do.

Pandas are a type of bear, but they seem more like raccoons or cats. In China, pandas are sometimes called *daxiongmao* (dah shee-ONG mah-oh), which means "Giant Bear Cat."

Like all bears, pandas are strong, intelligent animals with sharp teeth and a good sense of smell. Males weigh about 250 pounds and are about 4 to 6 feet long.

Pandas are great tree climbers. Sometimes they even sleep up in the treetops!

Bear Word

Habitat: An animal's natural home

Pandas have lived high in the mountains of China for millions of years. It is cold and rainy, but there are plenty of trees and a panda's favorite plant—bamboo.

Pandas used to live in more places, but today there is less open land with bamboo. Now pandas live in six forest habitats in China.

Panda Bodies

Pandas are black and white. This may help hide panda babies from predators, or enemies, in the snowy and rocky forest.

Their oily, woolly coat keeps them warm in the cold, wet forests where they live.

Hairs on the bottom of their feet keep them warm on the snowy ground.

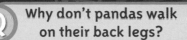
Their black eye spots may help them look fierce.

Just like cats, pandas can see very well at night, when they are most active.

Pandas have large teeth and strong jaw muscles that are perfect for crushing tough stalks of bamboo.

Bamboo Breakfast

Pandas spend their day sleeping a little and eating A LOT!

Bamboo for breakfast, bamboo for lunch, bamboo for dinner, and bamboo to munch. What do pandas eat? You guessed it— bamboo! It makes up almost all of a panda's diet.

Pandas have to eat 20 to 40 pounds of bamboo each day to stay alive. It takes 10 to 16 hours a day to find and eat all that bamboo!

A Day in the Life

Pandas mostly live alone. But sometimes they hang out in small groups.

Pandas use 11 different calls to communicate with each other. They also leave their scent on rocks and trees for other pandas to find.

Bear Words

Communicate: To pass on information

Scent: A smell. Pandas use scent to communicate.

Around August or September, a mother panda will find a den and give birth. Her newborn cub is about the same size and weight as an ice cream sandwich.

Panda cubs are pink, hairless, and blind at birth. They spend the day squeaking, crying, and drinking their mother's milk.

Bear Word

Cub:
A baby bear

Soon, black fur will grow around the cub's eyes and on its ears and legs.

Cubs stay with their mothers until they are about two or three years old.

1.

In a few weeks, the mother can leave her cub to find bamboo. The baby cries less and is able to keep itself warm.

2.

When a cub is about eight weeks old, it will finally open its eyes. But the cub still cannot walk until it is three months old.

3.

When the cub is six months old, it can eat bamboo, climb trees, and walk around, just like its mother.

Red Panda

When people think of pandas, they are usually thinking of the Giant Panda. But did you know there is another kind?

Red Pandas also live in China as well as other parts of Asia. They eat bamboo just like black-and-white pandas, but they also love roots and acorns. Red Pandas only grow to be about the size of a cat.

The Red Panda has red fur
and looks more like a raccoon
than a bear.

Protecting Pandas

Bear Word

Reserve:
Protected
land area

Today there are only about 1,600 pandas left in the wild. Many of the forests where pandas live have been cleared to make room for farms. Pandas have nowhere to go and no food to eat.

The Wolong (WOO-long) Panda Reserve in China is just one way people are trying to help. The 150 pandas that live there cannot be harmed.

0   500
Miles

C H I N A

□ Wolong Nature
Reserve

Panda Baby Boom

Pandas are also protected in zoos. The first pandas were brought to the United States from China in 1972. Today there are about 100 Red and Giant Pandas in zoos.

In just one year, 16 cubs were born at the Wolong Panda Reserve.

At first it was hard for Giant Panda moms to have cubs in zoos and on reserves. But in recent years, there has been a panda boom! Let's hear it for the cubs!

Earthquake!

In May 2008, a giant earthquake struck China. The center of the earthquake was right near the Wolong Reserve. Rocks the size of cars rained down from the steep mountains surrounding the pandas' home.

Now workers need to find new land for the pandas that lost their homes.

Bear Word

Earthquake: When the Earth's crust moves, it causes the ground to shake.

Panda-mazing Facts!

Did you know?

Ancient Chinese rulers kept pandas as their **pets!**

Pandas will **roll** around and tumble to get somewhere faster.

Pandas are very **shy** and will stay away from places where people live.

Q What do you get when you cross a playground with a bamboo forest?

A Panda-monium!

Pandas are **pink** when they are born! The color comes from their mom's saliva when she licks them. (Saliva means spit!)

Pandas can't run very fast, but they are good **swimmers** and great **tree climbers.**

Pandas can eat more than **22,000 pounds** of bamboo each year!

It takes **four years** to tell if a panda cub is a boy or girl.

Name That Bear

白豹

white leopard

白熊

white bear

猛氏兽

beast of prey

花熊

banded bear

Pandas can be found in Chinese stories and poems 3,000 years old! Over time, they have been called many different things. Which name do you think fits them best?

catlike bear

bearlike cat

white fox

great bear-cat

bamboo bear

HABITAT: An animal's natural home

COMMUNICATE: To pass on information

SCENT: A smell. Pandas use scent to communicate.

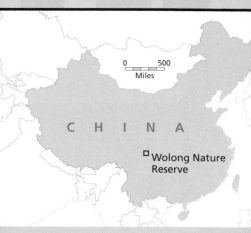

RESERVE: Protected land area

CUB: A baby bear

EARTHQUAKE: When the Earth's crust moves, it causes the ground to shake.

LEVEL
2

Dolphins

Melissa Stewart

NATIONAL
GEOGRAPHIC

Washington, D.C.

For Claire
—M.S.

Published by National Geographic Partners, LLC, Washington, D.C. 20036. All rights reserved.
Reproduction in whole or in part without written permission of the publisher is prohibited.

Library of Congress Cataloging-in-Publication Data
Stewart, Melissa.
Dolphins / Melissa Stewart.
p. cm.
ISBN 978-1-4263-0652-5 (pbk. : alk. paper) — ISBN 978-1-4263-0653-2 (library binding : alk. paper)
1. Dolphins—Juvenile literature. I. Title.
QL737.C432S73 2010
599.53—dc22

2009022832

Table of Contents

It's a Dolphin!

What swims
in the water,
but isn't a fish?

What whistles
and chirps,
but isn't a bird?

What loves to jump,
but isn't a frog?

It's a **DOLPHIN!**

Fish or Mammal?

A dolphin is a mammal—
just like you.

Dolphins have lungs and breathe air. They get oxygen through a hole on top of their heads.

Their tails move up and down.

They have soft, smooth skin.

A dolphin's body temperature is always about 97 degrees Fahrenheit.

OXYGEN:
An invisible gas
in air and water
that animals
breathe in.

MAMMAL:
A warm-blooded
animal that drinks
milk from its
mother and has a
backbone
and hair.

Dolphins look like fish, but they are different in some very important ways.

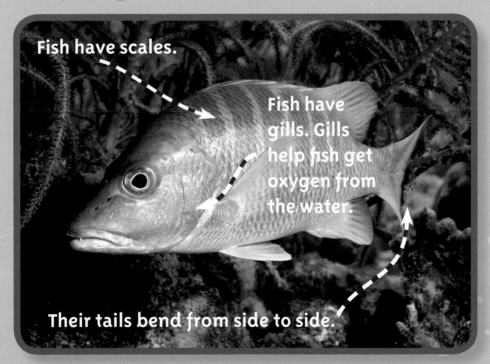

Fish have scales.

Fish have gills. Gills help fish get oxygen from the water.

Their tails bend from side to side.

A fish's body temperature matches the temperature of the water it's in.

A Dolphin's Life

A baby dolphin is called a calf.

A baby dolphin has a small mouth. The calf smacks food against the water to break it into bite-size bits.

A calf can swim as soon as it is born. It drinks milk from its mother's body. When the little dolphin is about six months old, it starts to eat fish.

Water Words

CALF:
A young dolphin

9

A dolphin pod

Dolphins live in small groups called pods. Some pods join together to form schools. A dolphin school may have more than 1,000 animals.

Dolphins use squeaks, squeals, and whistles to "talk" to each other. Some dolphins in a pod are in charge of watching for sharks and other predators.

Every dolphin has its own name. Each name is a series of whistling sounds.

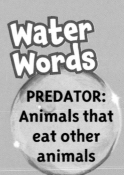

Water Words

PREDATOR: Animals that eat other animals

Dolphins work together to catch prey. Dolphin pods will swim circles around a school of fish until the fish are tightly packed together.

This big group of fish is called a "bait ball." When the fish have nowhere to escape, the dolphins take turns diving in for a snack.

Under the Sea

A dolphin's body is just right for life underwater.

Flippers help a dolphin start, stop, and turn.

The fin on a dolphin's back helps it stay balanced.

Its powerful tail pushes it through the water.

When a dolphin swims slowly,
it rises to the surface and breathes
once or twice a minute. When a
dolphin swims fast, it leaps out
of the water to catch its breath.

Blowhole

When a dolphin breathes out, air blasts out of its
blowhole at 100 miles an hour.

15

Dolphins have great eyesight, but the ocean can be very dark. It's hard for dolphins to see the little fish they like to eat on the ocean floor.

If a dolphin is hunting alone, it will put its head to the ground and make a clicking noise.

The noise hits anything in the dolphin's path and bounces back. A dolphin can find a fish by seeing it with sound!

This dolphin is using echolocation. You say it like this: eck oh low kay shun. Dolphins actually use echoes to locate the fish they can't see.

Where Dolphins Live

More than 30 different kinds of dolphins live on Earth.

Most dolphins swim in warm ocean waters near the Equator. But some live in cooler seas north and south of the Equator, and some even live in rivers.

The hourglass dolphin lives way out in the middle of the ocean.

The Hector's dolphin usually stays close to land.

Water Words

EQUATOR: An imaginary line halfway between the North and South Poles.

What's the Difference?

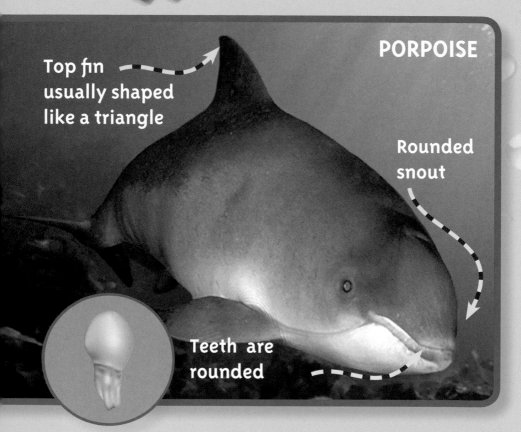

PORPOISE

Top fin usually shaped like a triangle

Rounded snout

Teeth are rounded

Have you ever seen a porpoise?
It looks like a dolphin, but it's
different. You say it like this: poor pus.

DOLPHIN

Pointed snout

Top fin usually hooked or curved

Teeth are pointed

A dolphin's body is longer and leaner than a porpoise's body. Dolphins are more curious and playful, too.

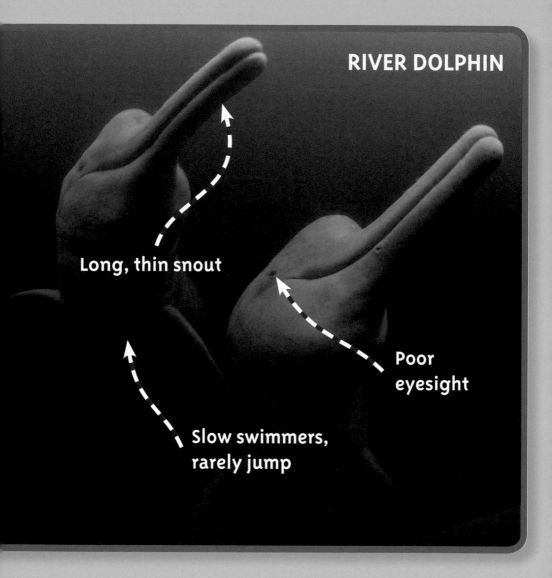

Long, thin snout

Poor eyesight

Slow swimmers, rarely jump

Have you ever seen a dolphin with a long pointy snout? This funny looking mammal is a river dolphin.

OCEAN DOLPHIN

Good eyesight

Short snout

Fast swimmers,
often jump

River dolphins are smaller than
their ocean-swimming cousins. They
are also less active and playful.

Super Dolphins

SUPER SPINNER

A spinner dolphin twirls through the air like a spiraling football. It can jump almost ten feet into the air and spin up to seven times.

Q What is a spinner dolphin's favorite amusement park ride?

A The merry-go-round.

EASY BREATHER

A dolphin spends most of its life holding its breath. A Risso's dolphin can go for 30 minutes without coming up for air.

DEEPEST DIVER

Whales and dolphins are very closely related. In fact, some animals we call whales really are dolphins. The long-finned pilot whale is a dolphin that can dive almost 2,000 feet!

25

The most amazing dolphin of all is the **ORCA,** also known as the killer whale. The orca wins almost every record-setting award in the dolphin category.

A killer whale can swim seven times faster than an Olympic swimmer!

Q What did the ocean say to the killer whale when it left on vacation?

A Nothing. It just waved.

HUNGRIEST
An orca eats everything from sea turtles and penguins to seals and sharks.

LONGEST LIVING
A killer whale can live up to 90 years.

BIGGEST
Males can grow almost as long as a school bus.

Goofing Off

Dolphins spend a lot of time hunting for food. And they are always on the lookout for danger. But sometimes dolphins just want to have fun. Dolphins make up all kinds of games.

PLAYING CATCH:
Toss seaweed into the air and try to catch it.

SURFING: Ride along storm waves or waves breaking near a beach.

TAG, YOU'RE IT: Chase each other through the water.

Dolphins and Humans

Dolphins are gentle, playful creatures. They are also very smart, which is why people and dolphins get along so well.

By learning about these friendly marine mammals, humans are helping to protect dolphins and the waters they live in.

CALF: A young dolphin

Equator

EQUATOR: An imaginary line halfway between the North and South Poles

MAMMAL: A warm-blooded animal that drinks its mother's milk, has a backbone, and hair.

OXYGEN: An invisible gas in air and water. It helps anima get energy from food.

PREDATOR: Animals that eat other animals

PREY: Animals that are eater by other animals

Cheetahs

Laura Marsh

NATIONAL
GEOGRAPHIC

Washington, D.C.

For Granny
—L. F. M.

Design by Yay Design

Paperback ISBN: 978-1-4263-0855-0
Hardcover ISBN: 978-1-4263-0856-7

CO = Corbis; GI = Getty Images; IS = iStockphoto.com; NP = naturepl.com; NGS = NationalGeographicStock.com; MP = Minden Pictures; SS = Shutterstock; cover, Chris Johns/NGS; 1, Manoj Shah/GI; 2, Michael Poliza/GI; 4 (top), Frans Lanting/Mint Images/GI; 4 (center), Roman Kobzarev/IS; 4 (bottom), Andrew Dowsett/S; 5, ZSSD/MP; 6 (left), Eric Isselée/SS; 6 (right), Eric Isselée/SS; 7 (top left), Panoramic Images/GI; 7 (top right), Hedrus/SS; 7 (left center), Jonathan and Angela/GI; 7 (right center), Frans Lanting; 7 (bottom left), Jonathan and Angela/GI; 7 (bottom right), Ivica Drusany/SS; 8 (left), Eric Isselée/IS; 8 (center), Eric Isselée/IS; 8 (right), Eric Isselée/IS; 8 (background), Gregor Schuster/GI; 9 (top), istvanffy/IS; 9 (bottom), Splurge Productions, Inc./GI; 10-11, Andy Rouse/NP; 12, Art Wolfe/GI; 13, Federico Veronesi/GI; 14, Martin Harvey/GI; 15, Anna Omelchenko/IS; 16-17, Superstock; 18 (top), Suzi Eszterhas/MP; 18 (bottom), Chris Johns/NGS; 19, Suzi Eszterhas/MP; 20-21, Suzi Eszterhas/NP; 22 (top), Albie Venter/SS; 22 (center), Suzi Eszterhas/MP; 22 (bottom), Suzi Eszterhas/MP; 23 (top), Federico Veronesi/GI; 23 (bottom), Acinonyx Jubatus/NP; 24, DAE Picture Library/GI; 24-25 (background), krechet/SS; 25, Robert Harding/GI; 26, Winfried Wisniewski/CO/GI; 28-29, Martin Harvey/Alamy; 30, Acinonyx Jubatus/MP; 31, Suzi Eszterhas/MP; 32 (top left), Art Wolfe/GI; 32 (top right), Simon King/NP; 32 (left center), Federico Veronesi/GI; 32 (right center), Francois Van Heerden/IS; 32 (bottom left), Suzi Eszterhas/NP; 32 (bottom right), Francois Van Heerden/IS

National Geographic supports K—12 educators with ELA Common Core Resources.
Visit natgeoed.org/commoncore for more information.

Table of Contents

It's a Cheetah!

What runs so fast
it races by in a flash?

What looks
like it cries
but has no
tears in
its eyes?

What is covered in spots
and lives where it's hot?

4

It's a cheetah! (And we're not "lion.")

Cheetahs are large cats that look as cute and cuddly as a house cat. But you wouldn't want to snuggle up to a cheetah!

Cheetahs are powerful hunters with sharp claws and teeth.

Spotting Cheetahs

Cheetahs and leopards look alike because they both have spots. But they are different in many ways.

Cheetahs have "tear marks." These are black stripes that run from their eyes to their mouths. Leopards don't have stripes on their faces.

Cheetah   # Leopard

T A I L

long and thin   thick and short

B O D Y

narrow   wide

H E A D

small   large

Safari Speedster

In a race between a lion, a greyhound dog, and a cheetah, which animal would win?

The cheetah, hands down!

The cheetah is the
fastest land animal on
Earth. It can reach
a running speed of
60 miles an hour in
just three seconds.
That's as fast as a
sports car!

What makes a cheetah so fast?
Its body is built for speed.

A long tail balances the cheetah when it makes sudden, sharp turns.

A flexible spine helps it change direction quickly.

Long legs help it run fast.

A thin, lean body helps it move quickly.

Word Bites

PREY: An animal that is eaten by another animal

Excellent eyesight makes spotting prey quick and easy.

Large nostrils let it breathe easily after running.

A small head makes the cheetah lighter.

Its claws don't completely pull back into its paws like other cats. The claws grip the ground when running, like cleats on a shoe.

Its deep chest makes breathing easier while running.

Great Hunters

camouflage
Say _CAM-oh-flaj_

Cheetahs are sneaky when they hunt! Their spotted coats act as camouflage in tall grass. They stalk their prey slowly and quietly.

When they get close, cheetahs chase their prey.

But cheetahs get tired quickly. Whew! They need to rest, too.

Word Bites

CAMOUFLAGE: An animal's natural color or form that allows it to blend in with its surroundings.

STALK: To move secretly toward something.

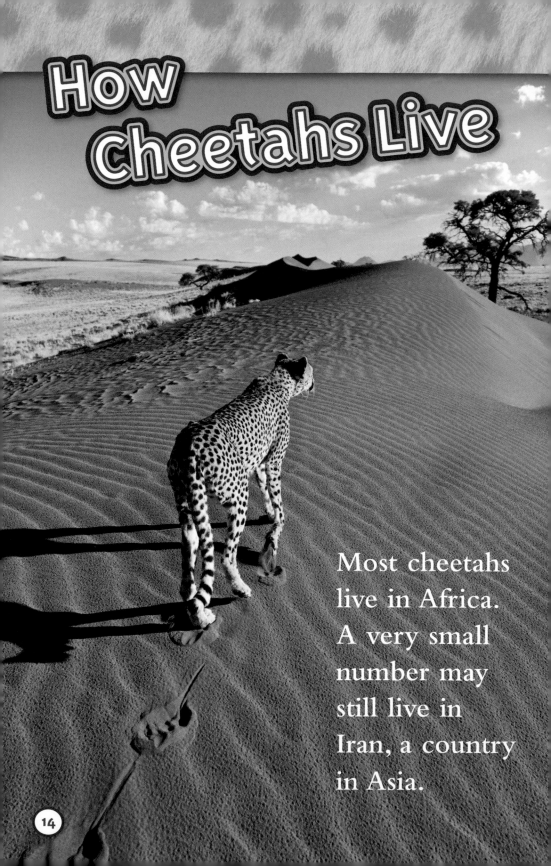

How Cheetahs Live

Most cheetahs live in Africa. A very small number may still live in Iran, a country in Asia.

Like people, cheetahs can live in different habitats. Cheetahs live on the savanna and in areas with lots of plants. They also live on grasslands and in the mountains.

But cheetahs can't live near crowded buildings. They need open space.

No matter where they live, male cheetahs stick together. Brothers live in a group called a coalition.

Female cheetahs live alone, except when caring for their cubs. Male and female cheetahs come together to have cubs. Then they live apart again.

coalition
Say *koh-ah-LISH-un*

Cubs

A mother cheetah has three to five cubs at one time. They are born blind and helpless.

But the cubs grow quickly! They can open their eyes and crawl in less than ten days.

The mother cheetah keeps the cubs safe in their den. If she needs to move, she carries them in her mouth.

Can you find the cheetah cubs?

The cubs' dark coats blend in with the shadows. The long, soft hair along their backs looks like the dry, dead grass.

The cubs are protected by camouflage. It's hard for predators to find them.

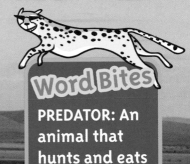

Word Bites

PREDATOR: An animal that hunts and eats other animals

Playing Around

The cubs learn a lot from their brothers and sisters. They wrestle, stalk, and chase one another.

They practice skills they will need for hunting when they grow up.

When the cubs are older, the mother cheetah teaches them to hunt. She also shows the cubs which predators to avoid.

Royal Cats

Statues of cheetahs from King Tut's tomb

Cheetahs have lived on Earth for a long, long time. As far back as ancient Egypt, pharaohs kept cheetahs as pets.

The famous pharoah King Tut was buried with many statues of cheetahs.

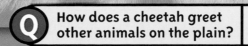

Some ancient Egyptians believed in a cat-goddess called Mafdet. They thought Mafdet could protect the pharaohs.

Art from ancient Egypt shows cheetahs on statues, furniture, and in paintings.

Mafdet
Say MAHF-**det**

Golden head of a cheetah found in King Tut's tomb

25

Cheetah Talk

Cheetahs make sounds that tell how they're feeling. Cheetahs can't roar like other big cats. But they can purr like a house cat.

Here's a dictionary for understanding cheetah talk:

Purring:
This is a low, motor-like sound, made when a cheetah is happy or content.

Bleating:
A cheetah bleats when it's upset. It sounds like a cat's meow.

Hissing:
When a cheetah feels angry or threatened, it may let out a sharp "h" sound.

Chirping:
Cheetahs chirp when they look for each other. The call sounds like a chirping bird.

Churring or stuttering:
During social meetings, cheetahs growl with a high pitch that stops and starts.

Growling:
A cheetah growls when it feels angry or threatened.

Saving Cheetahs

You need space to run, to jump, and to play—and so do cheetahs.

More people and more buildings push cheetahs onto smaller pieces of land. Cheetahs need lots of open space to live, to hunt, and to have babies.

Less open space means cheetahs are disappearing. Today fewer than 12,000 cheetahs live in the wild.

But some people are working to save cheetahs. And we are learning more about these big cats.

The more we know, the better chance we have to keep cheetahs on Earth.

Glossary

CAMOUFLAGE: An animal's natural color or form that allows it to blend in with its surroundings

HABITAT: The place where a plant or animal naturally lives

PREDATOR: An animal that hunts and eats other animals

PREY: An animal that is eaten by another animal

SAVANNA: A grassy plain with few trees in a hot, dry area

STALK: To move secretly toward something